Under the Sun

Futurepoem books   New York City   2003

Under the Sun
Rachel Levitsky

Futurepoem books
P.O. Box 34
New York, NY 10014
www.futurepoem.com

This edition first published in paperback by Futurepoem books
FIRST PAPERBACK EDITION

Opening quotes from: Benjamin, Walter. "Thesis on the Philosophy of History." *Illuminations*. Ed. Hannah Arendt. Trans. Harry Zohn. New York: Schocken Books, 1969. Notley, Alice. *Disobedience*. New York: Penguin Books, 2001.

Portions of this work have previously appeared in *eastvillage.com* and *Line Anthology*. Many thanks to Jerrold Shiroma who published an earlier version of this manuscript as an e-book on the Durationpress.com Web site.

The author acknowledges the many poets, friends who contributed critical comments and suggestions to this book. Special recognition goes to Lila Zemborain, Dana Greene, Carla Harryman, Camille Roy, Lauren Gudath, Beth Murray, Nicole Brossard, Renee Gladman, Nancy Ordover and Dan Machlin; all of whom are in here somewhere.

ISBN: 0-9716800-1-9

Design: Anthony Monahan

Body text set in Sabon and titles set in Trade Gothic.

Printed in the United States on acid-free paper by McNaughton Gunn.

Distributed by Small Press Distribution, Berkeley, California
Toll-free number (U.S. only): 800.869.7553
Bay area/International: 510.524.1668
Email: spd@spdbooks.org
Web: www.spdbooks.org

for Herbert Levitsky

Thinking involves not only the flow of thoughts, but their arrest as well.

—Walter Benjamin

There's always a third one, a third thing
What does *that* mean?

—Alice Notley

Contents

Prologue

(ocean/sky)

A photograph is taken of a sea or desert or rolling hillside or pasture of cloud. The clouds, first thick like drapery, break into puffy wisps. They are evenly distributed up here today.

There is logic to the pleasure of photographing these clouds. The photographs, because they will not be developed, are notable only in their absence. This last thought is lazy. The photographer who thinks it knows nothing about what she does. It's pretty is all. Quotidian. She loves that word in every language. So she imagines; since after all she doesn't know every language. The photographer is made of what she doesn't know. In the centuries in which she lives (there are three) the photographer fights with the philosophers.

Red in the face, always red in the face, with her right hand she gesticulates and shakes a small tight fist. She tries to grab one of them by the collar, the skinny, feeble one with glasses who wears always the expression of one who can't smile easily. Even he is lithe enough to escape her ferocity because with her other hand, the left, the photographer pushes him and the others away with a wave of her arm. This strange waving by her left hand is firm and aristocratic.

In her argument with the philosophers, she is not the lady who conquers them. Her beauty does not win them over. Though one becomes angry enough to go back at her, equally red in the face. He is macho, his name is Hans. His face gets up close into hers, pure with hatred. You are making no sense, he repeats. She returns—It's you, your abstractions, that make no sense and what's worse is you don't care. She is made calm by his fury, and continues—You're squeamish before the flesh that bore you, that you strive to bear into. She doesn't believe what she says, nor what he says. But because she fails his test, she knows he too is fundamentally wrong. She walks away, perplexed by the dream she is yet to have: of tunnels, caves and bridges, missing cities, failing to recognize the points of entry. She walks away, and looks for a way to go. Her way, she discovers, is in planes. She misses her enemy, who becomes a soldier, a job he hates from the moment he begins.

I. Landscrapes

"What is your favorite emotion?"
"Loss."
"Hare today, goner tomorrow."
"Shall we race?"

A Meeting, Not Upon Arrival

1.

Turtle sits and looks at Lady
Lady cannot return the
More-than-a-glance

2.

Turtle cannot read
The scene—her reflection
Blacked out on the

{eyes} (windows)

Lady falling asleep
How can Lady sleep
Urt puts her hand

In front of Lazy's eye
Lady awakes
Gasping for breath

1. Lady

A distraction.

She can't leave
easily—this room

In this room
The correspondence,

what's not easily left

2. Under the Moonless

Turtle herself
Apparent—in a physical way
Despite her absence

Which,
For the lady is
Physical, so

Gets on the plane
To make Turtle apparent
In a physical way

Turtle, physically away
Lady, not afraid
Of the play

1.

Urt's lady

is an invention

of a non-utopian

impossibility

At first kiss
Urt and Lazy
look away.
Should they? Name it

Why not.
The consequences.

[Sticking to it.
Hoping it will
Improve.]

2.

If the brain could be two

Instead   there is another

An ocean   an ocean,

So many

Hillocks

Eddies,

& mud.

This Isn't About Me / It's About Me
[You play your part, I'll play mine]

In a conversation
from which
what is remembered

Is what
each themselves
has said

II. Life Off the Farm

I went to hell today
so I know hell

What it is and
that I know it and

That I've returned
for more, to go back

and get some more

More than a season.
Hell is more than a season

Of the soul, the body
the earth's body

More than rotation, sleeping and waking and dreaming and forgetting
or remembering then forgetting quickly. Memory that challenge.
I remember hell perfectly well thank you. No need to apologize.
You two, the two of you, in hell too.

[Poised to say but frightened.]

"Penalty"

1.

Turtle has stolen pants
from the diner.
Knows when not to wear them:

Consequences !. !. !.
Everywhere
Frightened of the day

She will forget.

2.

Lady is losing.
Sinking her shoes
In snow [words]
        and mud [pictures].

Holes, the consequences
Apparent to turtles

Apparently Lazy
        is looking

For an improved means
Of transportation.

My Sunshine

An idea of heaven, silence there gray
Cloud movement quick without sound.

Days like that. When we are in them we question our existence, the
sound we watch exit our mouth, the sound staying stuck between our
ears. We doubt the reality of the couple, two hundred feet away even
when right upon them. Days like that. Days like heaven, even if we
are sad. We remember them and doubt the memory. We wonder if the
memory of heaven is memory in fact (of fact or dream).

[parables, aphorisms, metaphors,
word/pictures, word pictures]

No destination
but down. ⇩

———

No theory but seeds,
carried by birds,
to make weeds.

Lady,

takes herself

to the bar

order

to remember

what she is

capable of

[why every story
about women
sung

$.f.=.\text{♫}$ ♪.= □

to the tune
of virtue]

There is a bar/diner
on the corner

the same
corner
on every coast

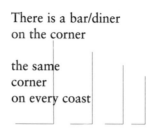

In some	bars/	diners
t	o	[
h	bj	o
e	e	b
	c	j
st	t	ec
o	s	t
o		
l	o	to
s	f	]

ENVY
AND
PIGEON
✖
l
o
n
g
i
n
g

A young, er . . .

Woman who
composed, in shades
of beige, birdlike

Plants herself
painters herself
into the picture

Sitting very straight

———

Pigeons
Trees
Slide into
a river
against a gray
curlicue/canvas.

———

Should they

Name names.

(Lady, Turtle, any other)

As positions on the
Floor/wall.

[No matter
what you call it]

Skies Are Gray

Airports, bus stations, underutilized working-class malls, random video
games floating in cavernous public space, their wires hanging and black,
cities without sidewalks—could be what is thought of as hell.

No noisier, no more colorful. Not more pleasurable nor busy than what
might be perceived as Heaven. It's you who has lost your thick skin.
Your veins, they show—down to the capillaries in your fingernails.
Look, here you are a red dog. Here you are blue.
.
.
.
.

Once upon a time when you flew.
Once upon a time before you doubted your agility.
Once upon a jigsaw puzzle that concealed the jigsaw path
        you were gliding upon.
At which age it hadn't yet occurred not to trust that which was bigger
        than you.
At which age your impulse was to protect that which was smaller.
When you believed you mattered to a thing if the thing mattered to you.
Whereupon your skin was intact, your genitals open.

. . . .

III. The White Canvas [Shoulder]

Silence

Makes the interpreter

Angry,

Angry to be

Angry.

                            Gallery filled with white and anger

She can't see the comfort of Burgundy or
Dark blue shaded by darker blue—
That which she likes to call

                                    Crow
                            Pigeon seen as
                                  Hawk

Gray against gray

Alliance

Makes her feel sad or

Ineffably hopeful

Febrile

With desire

Names it: N O U M E t U L W B M W W T D N S I M
(no one understands me except the unattainable lover who baffles me
with what she does not see
          in me.)

_____

_____
That black mess of scribbles with some red.

_____

Similar to silence
Ever more sinister

Sneakish ways it has
Infiltrating the
Otherwise
Laid-to-rest

Infuriating uninterrupted waste
Unloading it into the aura of the viewer.

(silent reading):

> *Plutonium, Microbes, Hydroflourocarbons, Benzine, Zinc, Phosphorus,
> Nitrates, Eutrophication, Vermin, Funk, Flies, Maggots, Chiggers, Lyme
> Ticks, Earwigs, Strep, Staph, Incest, Rabid Bats in the Attic, Pore Grease,
> DDT, PCBs, &tc.)*

> *As dust.*
> *Beautiful, from beginning to end.*

(Never Know, Dear)

Lady lifts herself up,   whether she can   Seeks (seeds)
gives away   or cannot perfect   (maple seed)
her pigeon stool   [perfect]   [theory]
spins and spins   a stumbling not   to break the fall.
                                as a child. Perhaps   Not now, later
                                she can fall   when she can fall

———

Turtle closes the diner. She cannot find her mood because it is the night
when there is not moon. She puts out a hand, looking for the lady.
Sees only dark hand. Lady is somewhere on a speeding plane. No pilot.

———

No destination
but down. ⇓

[returns, speaking:

The Writer of Prose

fills her space with

question marks

written as

statements, as

periods, a deception.

Makes her doubt

the names assigned,

the connections

formed with

epiphanies
from
the future.]

The Writer of Prose rejects the unknown; Knowledge isn't renewable resource, fossil fuel, petroleum, ozone, acid rain—though its transformations are acceptable, as a concept.

In her Book of Love the patients kick each other. All the lovers who enter quickly into the affair despite Lingering Doubt are committed to the Hospital where they have a chance to safely kick, slam bats into mats, scream at seemingly unsuspecting passersby.

In her Book of Love the consumers pose in front of backdrops visible only to the other viewers who will see: deception, naiveté, repetition, fear. The lover/consumer has a different view, through a false window of her own design, harmony, faultlessness, the healing power of her good love.

In her Book of Fantasy, Sexual and Other/wise, the writer of prose writes of bridges and tunnels, train stations, fast cars not moving, addiction.

The addicted who make search their occupation, are marked by erudition and swagger. Their music is very loud and makes them conspicuous to the neighbor. The neighbor is very loud which makes them the neighbor.

The Neighbor is always a problem. He asks questions but remains unmarked, unfixed. She marks him with her irritation. She makes him small. He is six feet five. He acts on a soap. He is an electrician who works at night. He stands in front of the door all day, smoking cigarettes. He drinks non-alcoholic beer. He is buff. He works out everyday, even on Sunday.

The stippled White Canvas makes the viewer, whose hand is trembling, who is now an addict, nervous, and angry to be nervous. Her erudition is now gibberish, interruption interpreted as high art by the spectators who cannot hear. No worry, the noise is visual. The addict is a wrack of nerve.

(She counts the chapters backwards, the neighbor moves quickly forward.)

———

IV. Arrangement [Mouth]
(In a Foreign Land You Are Permitted to Be Quiet)

Breakfast into the bottomless
pit. Food looks good
but doesn't taste good.

Everyone in the Room
pretending it's delicious.

Lady looks at them.

Words come off pages
Every text at once

a trail cannot—
can no longer—
be marked.

(Hansel and Gretel. Lady
sides with the witch and
never wears sun block.)

Turtle looks at Lady with twitch in the face. Search and paternal.
Dumbfounded confusion in Kodacolor. Compulsion. Squint to
understand the crooked and indeterminate method. Indefinite constant.
Purview::chaos.

Turtle seeks to be guided. Definition, not consequence. Seems to be

Something more permanent than bread crumbs.

(Why it is to Lady she looks
(Lady who seems to lend herself
(To whatever
(Notion of dream———invention

In the morning Urt says,

"I will write it
on a wall."

Turtle's wall
Lady's falter

She doesn't fault her,
tries to read the writing
on the wall. It's green.

———

Each night in her dreams Urt walks and sees: spectacles:

freezing people

the freezing of people

naked devils//sexy poses

sadism and postures filled

with Roman tents

a religious love

her lady screaming.

a third.

nameless.

ever-present.

———

                                        Beginning with contrast
                                        Urt holds her hand behind
                                                        her back
                                                     couples it
                                        with her other (diner) hand
                                        and places a knee on Lady

Thus holding Lady
raises the coupled fist
above her head and

                              brings it down.

Lady closes her eyes

          {windows}

turns her head

Feels something

on the inside

of her stomach

                         unusual this—
                           reaching in

                    hand without fingers
                    (shoulders without arms)

Lady clamps down

releases

births another.

Now there are three.

Sun Salutation

On your hands and knees
Head against the wall

My people, she says
There are things for which

Even we
Lose words.

Forever and ever
No joke and no wisdom

No relish in repetition
Or risk

Where is the food, the chair, the table
Where is my head, your hand, gravity

Where is there room
In this room,

Under the table
Beside the white

Bedspread

To Each Her Own

Four breasts meet
Eye to Eye
Not satisfied
With seeing

Wisdom isn't everything,
Nor beauty,
Nor being good,
Even particularly good

In bed—more
Vexation of the Spirit.
Lady is spirited and
Speedy

Turtle is tried by gluttony
Lady's gluttony
They speak without words
Without understanding a single

One. Turtle presses down on Lady.
Lady watches her now.

———

One day, or season
Leads to another. One arm
Turns into another.
Everything stops

At the third,
On the third day,
And the fourth.

Four days ago
Another four days to go.

They'll all go
To another city.

Lady clicking her heals
Falling into another.

V. Who Knows the Essence of a Thing Is Red and Cannot Be Duplicated Before Fading
[Shadowlife]

Three terms are necessarily uneven.
They are:
water and air and the boundary between the two
-you can see
-air presses against water
-the boundary hasn't got anything to say about it

There are two margins and a mass, one margin attached to the mass,
the other margin on the other side of the line, a thin red line, but it can
be black and/or blue. Speaking here of a country. The same could be
said for a page.

[Pull the narrative
into a visual scheme
disturbing and pleasing
harmonious study of color]

Lady is in the bar practicing learning. Learning is for ladies. Learning
for ladies is a practice of the negative, what not to become.

[i.e. I won't be bitter.]

I won't be bitter
I won't be bitter

(The neighbor . . . snoring)

Seasonal
[Deleted]

Each day has three distinct images in its rain [reign]

Driving in the rain
driving away the rain

At the highway ramp
Solitary man in black
Stiff standing
Under the rain

Over the highway bridge
Seagull flies all distant
Details immediately
Apparent
(despite their distance)

Off the exit a car
At the light
Next to it—a
K8 vehicle
(organ transport)

[disassembly]
[containment]

(the neighbor . . . snoring)

Town Square

When the air   surrounds its own boundary

　　　(underground)　　　　　　(rain)

　　　that　　　　　　is　　　　　　　　　　　　　　　light

　　　　　　　　　　　　　　　　　　　　　　　　　　　|

Theory　　　　　　　　　　　　　　　　　　　winter

house　　　　　train　　　　　plane　　　　sidewalk

　　　　once circular motion

　　　　　　one circular motion (remaining)

(underground)　　　　　　　　　　　(it's raining)

wind through windows//water through eyes

War outside
eyes inside

Coasts:
Horizontal:::::Vertical.....

Architectures of Knowing / Buildings on Shoulders /
Of Books No End but Weary Flesh

The verb pitch singing

For the critics (a bone, not a pome)
Refer to as: ego
in ego, out ego
in ego:
creatures
carrying in
their (cockroach)
house
for whom
the outside is the inside
boundary a given
get to seek the)pure(themselves
get backaches often

[This may be theory
broken into lines.
Unclear
if keeping it vague
makes it
poetry or theory.]

Around Turtle
_____ a line where she keeps the ground dry

Movement is this

serial positioning

of shots, flashes

In the Room

where there is no room

for negotiation

not negotiated_each particular position_ leaves a line
from which she, gets to simply see she
has become a little eyes-crossed from all these
havings of lines

Out egos for whom
self-definitions a compulsion
Self not as
something, as
something
negotiable
difficult to finish.

V A P O R

[Lady a sign of flesh weakened. By profusion of rooms, texts, tush.]

Verb bird, or is it bird verb

Rash, of the mouth

If she is me is you who is the me in this situation, is both confident
and embarrassed. Line of letters, plane of words. Some fiction. The
entire class now knows what they've been up to. Not messing around,
nor playing around, nor getting around—but needing a method for
this relationship which will make not mess the ego. I am the ego here.
Unfriendly ego one whose pleasures may be narrowly defined.

VI. The Map [The Words]

They are walking.

Lady sees a map under their feet.
She cannot believe its colors.

Fluorescent . . .

It is a sign.

She has been forgetting to notice signs or to believe in fortune. She is
willfully disobeying her rules. It doesn't matter, the path has been
sown, before or after.

It brings joy and tumult.

Urt smells her pits. They are stale diner. Fish. She doesn't yet eat fish.

Lady on the coast, her feet in the water.

Vanity as Turning Away
Lady bends Embrace

Turtle and Lady make a new contract. An occupation of looks and
resistance. To anything meaningful in speech. Once upon a time they
were stories. This one already written.

Civilizing repetitions
Competing repetitions

Turtle Believes
          in
Something New.

Pleasures

What is seen here

Does not implicate
The wanderer.

Less so when she lacks her camera.
Camera stolen. Voice too.

Lady implicated
Not corrupted.

Seen as corrupt. These clouds
They were once being painted.

Corrupting them
Painters who cannot help

Referring to
An accent on an image.

Sound corrupts the viewer
Unimplicated arms, complicated

Thick with muscle then
Legs, stronger than the arms.

We need here a new smell
Dirt , fat , pussy

The articulation of which
A sign of collaboration

War meeting art.

I Can See Clearly Now

I'm perfect, says Lady.
Perfected by what
Wasn't in fact
Lost. Was stolen

Hidden in storage
Far from corrupting eyes//.
Prison windows [ketchup smears.]

Appetite
Solution:

For the problem?

Say it isn't so.

VII. Indulgences: The Penitentiary [Desire!]

Destiny as a life written by the wall. on the wall. frescoed into
the concrete wall.
   acoustic break   repair
      wading pool
    cacophony in the city
      a rush
     who gets what

Here they are but has she cancelled yet. The plan.
The cats. The plane. Oops.

Positions by the wall. Urt back against it back rubbing, scratching,
climbing. Lady watching her, wanting to approach, wanting to be
aside, astride, wanting nothing behind or in front, but the body,
maybe a bed then. Inspiration, expiration. Some sort of belated,
bleating noise.

Don't look back . . .

Prisoners in position by the wall.
Repeated wall. Accident wall.
The wall.

Pink and green and gray today.

Interlude

Bounce in the morning, as though a poodle or a puppy. Messy mouthful.

Beware these confusions, choices of metaphor.

Hubris is the suspension of doubt.

[(Tell or not tell)]

Necessities

The carnival
has scattered

The mall
is red

The fire hydrant laying,
lying like mud

Lying in mud,
like a pillar

Ruin-ed. Is it
art then.

"A side of stolen pants
please?"

The storybook
in the newspaper.

Corrupted: she who
sees like this

Fucks little boys. Annoyed
by repetition version.

Dream. Because the neighbor
was snoring. Rain's end

At the boundary
where they meet.

Rooms lost and stolen
dirty under the desk.

The smell
the dead plants.

Erotica

She tries to place her hand up a tight ass.
It is a like putting a square peg in a round hole.
It can be done when her border stretches far enough.
But the ho' needs to want to stretch. (Canned laughter.)

This is the prison body. In bits and pieces.
Thank you for the eye. I'll hold it now.
Please though the day is late.
Decimate me. Decapitate me.

They don't meet here.

((*Here are the statues in the square*
        Here they are so we'll return
        The statue, the square, like the canvas, the house
        The statue, the bulge,
        Convex divisions in the wall, on the floor, twos and threes
        Mates that don't match
        Convex to point and line. division . by .
        Aluminum. .Plate...full - - - the missing red everywhere.
        Covered.by dark.by distance.by doubt.   ))

Phone lines/

Plane lines/

Eye line/

Ashes to Ashes / The Dead Who Are Dead

Turtle and Lady seen in the park sweating. They're sweet they are.

Today Lady will say nothing and ask forgiveness for her mean and
nasty thinking.

No one pays me with the life she leads.
No one pays me for my mean and nasty thinking.
No god strikes me down. No gods. No smear on my hand, my name.

I'll have some schmear.
I'd like some schmear.
Fear me. Tea? Hee.

[It's not funny.
nor particularly
skillful in language.
In fact there are no
word pictures here at all.]

Without a Trace

They keep
the emotions

quiet, so the animals
will feel less alone.

[Tina Darragh]

It's so sad
to be angry):/

Anger something
difficult to eat.

Everything is framed by two.
A couple formed by the shapes of their mouths.
Sucking sugar.
Everyone in the class knows what they want.
As two.
A living relic garden.

VIII. Place Value [Family Plans]

They're sorry
a little embarrassed.

And they will do it (ignorance)
again and again (bliss). It is the plan.

If Lady were to draw anger
it would have no lines
while being
entirely made up
of lines.

A little crowded
room of straights.

Then a room of
not straights. Each
like a scribble like

Face, on face, on
body. Line to
plane, train, of thought.

A reflecting pool of wet grass
oily images exchanged
in the sun.

Three of them in the dark room
playing a trick
picking up sticks.

They are not sticks
They are straws.

Turtle nearly wins

Then gives up.
Puts them back
where she'd found them on the floor.

For one this is windfall
        (Wind through straw.)
                        (Straw wrapped in plastic.)

For the other, pitfall
Hands tracing planes, counting legs, rattled by the
Train (Buried in rain.)

Defeat! Foolhardy explanations {heh} (heh, heh)

(Power, sensibility.) Greatness.   Gone.   Ghost.
Or is it, great ghost gone.
Gone great ghost?

Present Tense / The Factory

At the school of time and vision
the master paints one
identical painting each
day while
muted apprentices
consider

. . .

At the school of time and space in time
there is no paint.

Canvases are stretched
large or small.
There is great speed and
no hurry.

The school of time and light fills with water.
Well-lit and heavy, the water, carrying so much death and light.
Rocks, birds, branch, the painter, backdrop: container.
The origin of thought gone missing. Repetitions scheduled.

At the school for change painters have two rooms each.
In one there is an icy drag queen whose bare back is
what is seen by mothers.
The other is brother and
natural scenery. The curves entwined.
All mouths open. The motion:
opening doors.

At the school for memory and longing, their eyeballs settle in the center
of their face. They are eyes crossed with desire to recall gesture and the
angle of light on the wall behind. Their one hand is high, atrophied

by the repetition, the effort to repeat it well. With the other, photos are taken on three planes of space: close, far and farther.

At the school for utopian conditionals they imagine the unheard sounds which imagine themselves as paintings or pictures that can be photos— or a moment framed simply by the eye. Pictures that can only be read inside the head. Real though, though this story is not.

At the school of schools the laughter is fabulous.
The experts delight in themselves,
at their elimination
of the neighbor.

The Wall / Against the Wall / Camouflage Theory

Not a predator, but homeless. A slow cloud mackerel sky.
Seasons erased.

Living in picture theory. Likes and likes in which a couple who walk
down the street wear unremarkable clothing. No man stops them, to
take a picture that will later be used for pornographic purpose.

On the train they don't need to be gendered when they are watching,
though cannot control who genders them, especially the one of them
with lipstick and a red shirt tight over ample boobs.

Ungendered and watching themselves they are looking at different
things, though not necessarily looking at them differently: how one is
good-looking; how the sexy one isn't that same one.

How much the luscious breast flesh with tattoo contributes!
Annihilates certain effects: aging and acne. How the one next to her
who is quick to hostility hasn't got gender, 's got no gender at all.

Audience

yes

for want of story

[my fault
all these
characters—
insulting, really]

besides, the facts
which keep changing

the shower not taken
was a bath in which

they were not together

besides, it was not them
there was another, and another

their colors
brown, white, beige

(the skin, the floor)
        (the bath, the robe)
                (the skin, the dawn)
        (the bath, the skin)
(the dawn, the floor)
        (the bath, the floor)
                (the robe, the dawn)

(the wall, the diner, the neighbor, the school) (stool) (Pigeon)
(the moon, poodle) Fish.

Foam. Addiction. Corner.

[Between Benjamin,
Brecht, Beckett—
brackets
my feminine problem.]

———

Turtle doesn't like the weather
all the time—so we can say it
in the affirmative   simple   present:
Turtle likes the weather
some of the time.

[I value the idea
of writing
about writing
in writing—
poetry is the vaguest
of writing, I haven't got
the vaguest idea
how to fix that]

If the book
on the table
has (the evidence of) a stain
is it not (caused by) the fault
in the Turtle

If it is not the fault
of the Turtle
the blame is cleaved
now married, cleaved
now kaput.

IX. Overlay [Garments, Ointments]

What's bare
becomes messy
when annihilated
by (white) cover
though its remarkable
movement to
and from (toward :: away)
original vision
something seen.

As bib (spider)
in place of baby.

Baby (FOAM)
with the bathwater.

A word from the wise.

(Get off the field.)

––––––

♫ Everything is beautiful. ♫

––––––

Loud Lady, Her Majesty

Straight backed
wide falling
thumpingly solid
opaque resistant
demanding restraint
Wide in the eye
Big in the belly
Vague, exacting
consistent, disruptive
untrained indulgence

Fresh—resistant
to the impact of THINGS
while indulging.

Emperor Ur

Supine her position
Supreme her adjective
Mirth her emotion

E tells Lady to obey her Turtle
and Lady sings, "You know I did,
You know I did, You know I di...hid."

then

"How silly you are."

or

"How could you?"

E is often shifting
her mind,
                    position.

or

Exchanging positions
inside her mind.

Doesn't think of it
as flirting. Thinks

Busy. Occupies a middle
to/in Lazy's muddle.

The Rock, the Island

Mouth product (talk) becomes enemy. Erasing Lady.
Urt under the rock of it, shady. Forgetting Lady, getting ragey.

They meet their abstractions in the flesh. They live in the house. Gray
(against gray) is placed into a boundary of wall. (The wall boundary.)
Curved or straight, descending point and line, between what and what
was said. Productive issue of control, emperor Turtle. (Corners recreate
confusion.) Glass or skin. Control of self or control of lover. Or
controlling each other, like painting. The fingers treated as brushes, the
sand which gets in the paint. Liver. Bodily.

If she could do again. As FOAM. To ocean. FOAM to her hair (not
her head). She put her hand there. She did, she did. A weight as
flighty as air.

Under the Rock

Angry and angry to be angry
missing her salty dog
her diner stench
the sun is warm the window wide
her face unchanged, unchanging
in the light, on the picture
though she's changed, is charged
is charging
to be put in charge
in the picture
by high-end scribbles
(revelatory)
and cheap scribbling over
a well lit dark one.

Mother Love

My dear I have a confession to make *I do not want* to leave the
confines of *my body* though its limits almost predictable the mind is so
much so galactic *my body's* absorptive remarkable do not punish for
the sound okay though the cost *I* understand *Infidelity*.

The body determines the limits of recherché.
I do not wish beyond it I want you there
                                    just beyond it.

X. Shiva [Display, Folly, Magnificence]

the pigeons:

a reflecting pool

rotating carrying flipping

one-thousand feet

into the sky

plane above ✈

the shimmer

of birds

low, slow

↗ clumsy ↘

Ghost Off Her Coast

From the plane
Lady walks out onto a thousand clouds &
Drops onto Turtle's city
Trying to get to
One lovely spot where
Once there was Sun.

Having flown cannot return
to the ground.
Hovers, perpendicular?

Or is it adjacent,
(head cocked)
Next to but upright
Foot down. Has
seen it from above
from the map
below her, the feet.

Below the feet lines like scribble, above the steps, the stages, the world
stage. One in a circle and then in the blind spot the thing that is surprising,
the boundary experience won't define, pipelines, witch fisheries, the spout,
the singular train, the stop line of the rain, the train behind the singular
train, the race, the boats racing.

Arrives alone like the rain, arrives again the rain passover, passes over.

Lady's coast is made for return. Urt's for yearn.

The Clouds

Infinitely more
Intimidating on
Lady's coast
Where ladies wear high
Heals and black frocks,
Where suddenness,
Difficulty, the unhappy up close
Repertoire.

Her dream: Turtle bald,
In the corner, mean, reptilian.
Rising   fucking   kissing
On the way out the door
One mean look back
Pillar of salt thinks Lazy
Please turn her into a pillar of salt

not be bitter
not be bitter

The Way We Were

Titters to what love means, an idiom/an excessive
hysterical overload of language

> *How were we? Oh, happy,*
> *I guess,*
> *one at a time that is.*

Turtle and Lady resist physical violence.
For some reason.

Two and two makes three:
)hair on the chest
)hair on the head
)hair on the chest

Like names like "destiny"
Unlike without it
-repelled by the ideational violence of the concept
-a thing that is nothing but a feeling
-which produces nothing and destroys feeling

But to see them
Like packs of street dogs

In step, in light step
In the light of their step
In light of steps. Up up up.

Lady crouches in the dark
Rolls over, flicks genitals.

Dubious notion:
the advantage of three

can we help it,
someone somewhere
narrates by singing

———

Our love is
Like a ship on the ocean

———

Lady is a line in a threefold cord
quickly and tactlessly broken

Her maps are as nothing:
paper on paper on paper

As gender, absent or multiple
live, torture

Or pissing against the wall.
The breast is beautiful.

What constitutes (thought of)
as the present.

Blank Canvas

Night
Mutes activity
Lady isn't part of.

Activity
Mutes Lady's nights.

She tries.
She gets tired.

Neither body,
Nor mind

Green
against green
Black

against black
Misty

Small gray spot
behind which

Men die, snakes
emerge wakefully.

The magical thinking place.

✄

The maneuverer of time, of space, is crooked.

XI. Light Is Sweet [Though Mirth Is for Fools, Nothing Is Better]

As two they are one are slippery are ennui.
As two they have rules have neighbors.
Every cloud a choice between
Selling and suffering/ . . . /

Every painting the same
Shift, of time, of color
Magical realignment of space
Exaggeration of singular bodies
Body type bodies

The lack of evidence
Here, in this story-poem
Will show
It doesn't actually happen,

Though there is music
In their heads' morning
Music whose source is
Unnamable. In their

Heads, mornings
Not simultaneous
Mornings which are
Equally confusing.

A twisted effort to
Report their musings
As dreams. Dreams
Whose tracks are evident
In fossil-studded morning songs.

Crises

Upon crisis

The city
Built in a day
On desert

Where
A city
Lasts

For its day.

Upon a crisis
of stone,

a growth
as lovely
as lichen,

a profusion
over abundance
exaggeration of memory
indicating

Travel.

Steppe::
Turtle's complicated Dark
Where a spider (scared her)
(sitting down) (besides her)

A land questioned

Not turned toward
Nor seen.

The divinity of destiny
of destruction. Ruin-ed

Misnamed
the third   a
praying mass

Which wanting
cannot be numbered
nor named

Which
while massing

Incapable
of regret

[Glad to buy that expensive.]

The Neighbor

Brothers and sisters
black and white
poor and gilded surfaces
where the sky is close
The half moon
least remarkable

So unsentimental
it needn't be hidden

Looking closely the
veil of blue obscure
the other half at
a distance hidden
from irresistible sins
of the other

irrepressible brother's
bare back speaks
(   )

XII. A General Levity
[Ashes, Dust, a Conch Shell for One]

The peaches and blues
are appealing and
distrusted by
her academicians
who insist upon
red shoes with their
red pants.

On the other hand,

        the urban sun

        is a trickster!

                sent

                  by the whales
                  as they

        flip
        ships.

There is much
we can say
about fracture.

Who amongst us
doesn't sell /:) (:/
consorts with neighbor / (: :) /.

Why we bother.

The Third Room
[Masturbation scenery]

Laughing and crying:
you know it's the same release.

"Why do you say that?
You, who are not unbeautiful and hold
So much promise. Why are you

Acting this way?"

She doesn't know

This room

        Which promises
                Ocean
                    Sky

Love?

Is the room beautiful?
Kind of bare and/or messy/shattered

                Blue. Livid.

Epilogue

In a foreign country, the photographer meets the soldier. He smiles at her as one who is happy to see someone. She stops herself from looking behind her shoulder at someone else the soldier could be smiling at. Smiling, he is adorable, so she concentrates in order to remember his rage and her resistance. When she returns to smile back finally willing to move towards him, he's gone.

Addictions and Neighbors

"i wanna be fucked"
"i wanna be fucked up"

Mother Load

Unrequited love is the story of one knowing she knows what for the other is only a fantasy of knowing. Shaken by the blow (dreamy).

Continue dreaming an escalation of crumble. Continue dreaming your walking increases color increases density color increases. Continue walking.

The white, the black, a boundary. What a dream tells (in real time) differs from the phantom state of walking. What a scene tells.

ignorant. of the body. before